"The discovery of a new dish does
more for the happiness of mankind
than the discovery of a star."

Anthelme Brillat-Savarin

This edition © Robert Frederick Ltd. 1996
Old Orchard Street, Bath BA1 1JU, England

Printed in China
by Man Sang Envelope Mfg. Co . Ltd

The Food Lover's

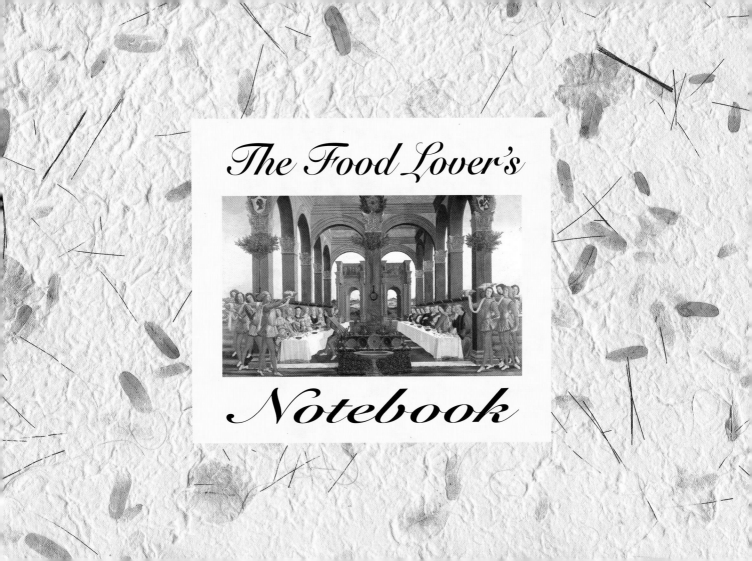

Notebook

Kitchen Information

TEMPERATURE CONVERSION CHART

°F	°C
212B	100B
122	50
113	45
104	40
95	35
86	30
77	25
68	20
59	15
50	10
41	5
32	0
23	-5
14	-10
5	-15
-4	-20

*Conversions given are approximate.
Never mix metric and imperial measures in one recipe – stick to one system or the other.*

LIQUID TEMPERATURES
(water, milk, etc)

Boiling Point	100°C	212°F
Simmering	96°C	205°F
Tepid	37°C	96°F
Freezing Point	0°C	32°F

COOKING (DIAL MARKINGS)

Gasmark	¼	1	2	3	4
Fahrenheit	250	275	300	325	350
Celsius	120	140	150	160	180

Gasmark	5	6	7	8	9
Fahrenheit	375	400	425	450	475
Celsius	190	200	220	230	240

OVEN TEMPERATURES

Gasmark	Description	Gasmark	Description
¼	Very Slow	4	Moderate
½	Very Slow	5	Moderately Hot
1	Slow	6	Moderately Hot
2	Slow	7	Hot
3	Moderate	8	Hot
		9	Very Hot

DRY WEIGHT

Approximate gram conversion to nearest round figure	Recommended gram conversion to nearest 25g	Imperial ounce (oz)	
28	25	1	
57	50	2	
85	75	3	
113	100-125	4	(¼ lb)
142	150	5	
170	175	6	
198	200	7	
227	225	8	(½ lb)
255	250	9	
284	275	10	
311	300	11	
340	350	12	(¾ lb)
368	375	13	
396	400	14	
425	425	15	
453	450	16	(1lb)

LIQUID MEASURES

Approx. ml conversion*	Recommended ml equivalent	Imperial pint	Imperial fluid ounce (oz)
568	575-600	1	20
284	300	½	10
142	150	¼	5

* to nearest round figure

Herbs

Herbs play an essential role in any kitchen, adding flavour and distinction to many dishes. All are available fresh or dried but remember that fresh herbs have a milder flavour and use roughly 15ml (1 tablespoon) of fresh herbs to 5ml (1 teaspoon) of dried.

Basil (Ocimum basilicum)
Two types of basil are grown; sweet and bush. The former is the more common and has largish, shiny, green leaves and a strong but sweet flavour. It is one of the best herbs to add to tomatoes, eggs, mushrooms and pasta dishes, forms part of a classic bouquet garni, and is an essential part of pesto sauce. Basil does not dry very successfully.

Bay Leaves (Laurus nobilis)
Sweet bay or bay laurel is a Mediterranean tree. The leaves are shiny, smooth and dark with a strong aromatic scent. It is often added to stocks when poaching fish, to marinades, casseroles, soups and stews. It can also be used to flavour milk puddings.

Chervil (Anthriscus cerefolium)
Chervil is a member of the parsley family and is very popular with French chefs. It has a fern-like leaf, offering a delicate taste with a hint of anise. It is especially good in soups, egg and cheese dishes, or added for flavour to green salad. It can also be used as a garnish.

Chives (Allium schoenoprasum)
A member of the onion family, chives have a mild onion flavour and long, spiky, green leaves. Raw chives are frequently used in salads, but can be added to omelettes, cheese dishes, and, mixed with soured cream, used as a topping for baked potatoes.

Coriander (Coriandrum sativum)
Coriander has flat feathery leaves and is often confused with flat parsley. It has a distinctive spicy flavour and is popular in Southern European, Indian and South East Asian cooking. The leaves are chopped and added to curries, stews, soups and marinades. It is also known as Chinese or Japanese parsley, and is used in the same way as parsley.

Dill (Anethum graveolens)
Dill is a delicate, feathery herb with an aromatic, sharp but sweet flavour. One of the most popular herbs in Scandinavia, it is especially good with fish if added to the marinade, cooking liquid or accompanying sauces. It can also be added to vegetables, cream or cottage cheese.

Lemon Balm (Melissa officinalis)
The crushed leaves of this plant give off a wonderful lemony scent, making them ideal for use in salads.

Marjoram (Origanum majorana)
Sweet marjoram, a Mediterranean plant, has small, furry leaves and a flavour similar to oregano but sweeter and milder. It can be added to most savoury dishes and is good with marrow, potatoes and rice. It is fragrant and can be dried successfully.

Herbs

Mint (Menta spp.)
There are many species of this popular herb, from spearmint to the fresh-tasting peppermint used for tisanes. It is probably the best known herb in Britain and most commonly used with lamb and new potatoes. It can also be added to other young vegetables or chopped with minced beef, or mixed with yogurt for a dip. It also combines well with fruit.

Oregano (Origanum vulgare)
Oregano is wild marjoram, and, as it has the best flavour if grown in strong sun, is popular in Mediterranean cuisines. The flavour is similar to marjoram but stronger and the leaves are larger and darker. It enhances many meat dishes and it is often added to salads, pizza and tomato based dishes. Oregano can be dried successfully.

Parsley (Petroselinum crispum)
There are two types of parsley: curled and flat. Flat (or French) parsley is generally grown in Europe and is considered to have a finer taste than curled parsley, but both are strong in Vitamin C and iron. Parsley is an essential part of a bouquet garni. It enlivens most savoury dishes and is often simply used as a garnish, either chopped or as sprigs. The chopped leaves can be added to salads, soups, sauces and cooked vegetables. If chewed after eating garlic it should remove the smell.

Rosemary (Rosmarinus officinalis)
A pungent, fragrant shrub with small, narrow leaves, set densely on the branches. It is often used with lamb but can be used with other meats and in vegetable dishes such as ratatouille or added to marinades.

Sage (Salvia officinalis)
Sage comes in many varieties and is a strongly flavoured herb with narrow, pale grey-green leaves with a rough texture. It has traditionally been used with pork, liver, and in stuffing, but can be used with any richly flavoured meat, and in cheese and tomato dishes. It dries well but can become musty if kept too long.

Savory (Satureja)
There are two varieties of savory: winter and summer. The German name for winter savory means "bean-herb", indicating its traditional use, while summer savory is similar and even more aromatic.

Tarragon (Artemisia dracunculus)
There are two varieties of this herb: French and Russian. The French variety is harder to grow but is far more aromatic than the Russian. It has a distinctive flavour and shiny narrow leaves. It is widely used in vinegars, soups, stuffings, sauces, and salad dressings, and is also good with roast meat, poultry dishes and fish.

Thyme (Thymus vulgaris)
This popular herb contains an essential oil, thymol, which helps to digest fatty foods. Its small, dark-green bushy leaves have a very strong flavour. It is another herb which should be used in a bouquet garni, and it can be used to flavour meat, fish, soups, stews and vegetables.

Spices

Spices are the dried parts of aromatic plants and may be the fruit, root, flower, bud, bark or seed. For the best flavour, grind your own spices just before use.

Aniseed (Pimpinella asinum)
Aniseed has a strong liquorice flavour and is popular in Mexico and all over the Mediterranean.

Capers (Capparis spinosa)
The buds of a small Mediterranean bush, these are usually sold pickled in vinegar and should not be allowed to dry out. While used mostly in sauces and salads, they are also popular as a pizza topping, adding an authentic Mediterranean flavour.

Cardamom (Elettaria cardamomum)
Cardamom is a relative of the ginger family, available both whole green, black or white or ground. The most common is the grey-green pod which contains minute, dark brown seeds with an unmistakable bitter-sweet flavour with a hint of lemon and eucalyptus. It is used extensively in sweet and savoury Indian cookery as well as in Europe and the Middle East for cakes, biscuits and pickles and to flavour drinks.

Chili (Capsicum frutescens)
Ripe chili peppers dry and keep well and are most commonly used in chili powder. Cayenne is a very hot, pungent red chili sold ready ground. Milder chili powders can be found or you can use chili seasoning which is a blend of ground dried chilis with other spices. It is used (sparingly) in meat, fish, poultry and egg dishes as well as soups, sauces and pickles.

Cinnamon (Cinnamomum zeylanicum)
The distinctive sticks of dried bark are harvested from the young shoots of a large, tropical evergreen. While best purchased as sticks and used whole or ground, it is also available as a powder and has a sweet pungent flavour. It is usually added to savoury dishes in the East and to sweet dishes in the West such as apple desserts, cakes and mulled drinks.

Cloves (Eugenia caryophyllata)
Cloves are the unopened flower buds of the tropical clove tree. They turn a rich brown when dried and resemble small nails. Cloves have a penetrating taste and are available whole or ground: if used whole then they are best removed before a dish is eaten. Use to flavour fruit dishes, mulled wine, mincemeat, bread sauce and curries.

Coriander (Coriandrum sativum)
Coriander is a member of the parsley family. The aromatic brown seeds have a sweet orangey flavour. Sold whole or ground, they are quite mild so can be used fairly freely and are used widely in Arab and Eastern cookery; in curries, casseroles, soups, couscous and hummus and with vegetables and chutneys.

Cumin (Cuminum cyminum)
Cumin is a member of the parsley family and is available both as seeds

"There is no love sincerer than
the love of food."

George Bernard Shaw

Spices

or powdered. It has a sharp, spicy, slightly bitter taste and should be used in moderation. Often combined with coriander as a basic curry mixture, it is also used for flavouring Middle Eastern fish recipes, casseroles and couscous. It can be added to pickles, chutneys, soups and rice dishes.

Ginger (Zingiber officinale)
Ginger is a distinctive knobbly root with a hot sweetish taste sold in several forms. Fresh root ginger, essential for many Eastern recipes, releases its true flavour on cooking. It is peeled and then sliced or grated for use in curries, Chinese cooking or marinades for meat, fish and poultry. Dried ginger is the dried ground root and is best used in preserves, cakes, biscuits and puddings. Stem ginger is available preserved in syrup or crystallized and is a sweetmeat either eaten whole, with carel, or used in breads, cakes, confectionery and desserts.

Mace (Myristica fragrans)
Mace is the dried outer membrane of nutmeg. It is sold both as blades or ground, although ground mace quickly loses its flavour. It is used in mulled wines and punches, meat pies, loaves, stews, savoury white sauces and in milk puddings.

Nutmeg (Myristica fragrans)
Nutmeg has a brown uneven outer surface with a pale interior. It is milder than mace although slightly nuttier and is widely available whole or ground, but as it loses its flavour quickly, is best grated as required.

It can be sprinkled on vegetables and is used in soups, sauces, meat terrines, pates, and puddings.

Paprika (Capsicum annum)
A finely ground red powder made from the fruits of several chili plants, popular in Hungary and Spain. The flesh only is used for mild sweet paprikas whilst the seeds are included in more pungent paprikas. Use to add colour to egg and cheese dishes, in salads, with fish and shellfish, chicken and classically in Hungarian Goulash.

Saffron (Crocus sativus)
The dried stigmas of the saffron crocus flower, saffron is expensive, as it is individually handpicked, and imparts a slightly bitter honey-like flavour and a yellow colour. It is safer to buy the threads as the powder is easy to adulterate. Add to rice dishes, Paella, Bouillabaisse and Cornish Saffron cake.

Turmeric (Circuma longa)
Turmeric is the dried root of a plant from the ginger family, usually sold ground, although sometimes sold fresh. It has a strong woody aroma and a slightly bitter flavour and is used to colour rice, pickles, cakes and in curries and dhals. It is sometimes used as a cheap substitute for saffron to colour dishes, but the flavour is not the same.

Vanilla (Vanilla planifolia)
Vanilla is the fruit of a Mexican orchid plant. It is traditionally used to flavour chocolate, and is good in many sweet dishes, though expensive.

Food & Health ~ Calorie Counting

Calories per ounce (25g)
unless otherwise stated:

Anchovies	40
Apples	10
Apricots	
Canned in syrup	30
Dried	50
Fresh, with stone	5
Artichokes (boiled)	5
Asparagus	5
Aubergines	5
Sliced & fried (1oz raw)	60
Avocado Pears (flesh only)	65
Bacon	
Back raw	120
Streaky raw	115
Bananas (flesh only)	20
Bass (steamed fillet)	35
Bean Sprouts (raw)	10
Beans	
Baked beans	20
Broad (boiled)	15
Butter (boiled)	25
French (boiled)	negligible
Haricot (boiled)	30
Kidney (canned)	25
Runner (boiled)	5
Soya (raw, dried)	115
Beef	
Brisket (boiled)	90
Minced beef (raw)	75

Minced beef (1oz raw, well fried & drained of fat)	45
Rump steak (fried, lean)	55
Rump steak (grilled, lean)	50
Sirloin (roast, lean & fat)	50
Stewing steak (raw)	50
Topside (roast, lean & fat)	60
Beetroot (boiled)	15
Blackberries (fresh)	10
Blackcurrants (fresh)	10
Black Pudding (raw)	105
Bran	60
Bread	
Brown/Wheatmeal/Hovis/White	65
Malt	70
Wholemeal	60
Bap (50g)	120
Croissant (50g)	270
Crusty roll	145
French Bread (50g)	130
Granary	70
Hot cross bun (50g)	180
Pitta bread (45g)	125
Rye bread	70
Tea cake (50g)	155
Broccoli (boiled)	5
Brussels Sprouts (boiled)	5
Butter	210
Cabbage (boiled)	5
Carrots (boiled)	5
Cauliflower (boiled)	5
Caviar	75

Celery	negligible
Cheese	
Austrian Smoked	80
Babybel	95
Blue Stilton	130
Boursin	115
Brie	90
Cairphilly	120
Camembert	90
Cheddar	120
Cheshire	110
Cottage Cheese	25
Cream Cheese	125
Curd Cheese	40
Danish Blue	105
Danish Mozzarella	100
Double Gloucester	105
Edam	90
Emmenthal	115
Gorgonzola	110
Gouda (not matured)	95
Gruyere	130
Lancashire	110
Leicester	105
Norwegian Blue	100
Parmesan	115
Processed	90
Rambol (with walnuts)	115
Roquefort	90
Sage Derby	110
Wensleydale	115
White Stilton	95

Food & Health ~ Calorie Counting

			Raw	Fried
Cherries		Roast, meat, fat & skin		95
Fresh with stones	10	**Eggs (Graded)**	**Raw**	**Fried**
Glace	60	1	95	145
Chicken		2	90	140
On bone, raw	25	3	80	130
Meat only, raw	40	4	75	120
Meat & skin, roast	60	5	70	110
Chinese Leaves	negligible	6	60	100
Chives	10	Yolk of size 3 egg		60
Chocolate		White of size 3 egg		15
Milk/Plain	150	**Gherkins**		5
Cooking	155	**Gooseberries** (fresh, dessert)		10
Cod		**Grapefruit**		
On bone, raw	15	Canned in syrup		15
Fillet, raw	20	Flesh only/With skin		5
Fried in batter	55	Juice		10
Steamed fillet	25	**Grapes**		15
Coffee (instant)	30	**Haddock**		
Corned Beef	60	On bone, raw		15
Corn o/t Cob (boiled, kernels only)	35	Fillet, raw		20
Courgettes	5	On bone, smoked		20
Cream		Smoked fillet		30
Clotted	165	Fried fillet in breadcrumbs		50
Double	125	**Hake**		
Single	60	On bone, raw		10
Soured	55	Fillet, raw		20
Whipping	95	Fillet, steamed		30
Cucumber	5	Fillet, fried		60
Currants	70	**Halibut**		
Dates (per date)	15	On bone, steamed		30
Duck		Fillet, steamed		35
Roast, meat only	55	**Ham**		

Lean, boiled	60
Fatty, boiled	120
Herring	
On bone, grilled	40
Fillet, grilled	55
Honey	80
Ice-cream	45
Jam	75
Kidney (raw)	25
Kippers (baked or grilled fillet)	60
Lamb	
Roast breast, boned,	115
Roast breast, boned, lean only	75
Roast leg, boned,	75
Roast leg, boned, lean only	55
Roast shoulder, lean & fat	90
Roast shoulder, lean only	55
Leeks (raw)	10
Lemon Sole	
On bone (grilled or steamed)	20
Fillet (grilled or steamed)	25
Lentils (boiled)	30
Lettuce (raw)	5
Liver	
Chicken's, fried	55
Lamb's, fried	65
Ox, stewed	55
Pig's, stewed	55
Liver sausage	90
Lobster	
With shell, boiled	10
Meat only, boiled	35

Food & Health ~ Calorie Counting

Macaroni (boiled)	35	Olives (with stones, in brine)	25	Pineapples	
Mackerel		Onions		Fresh	15
On bone, fried	40	Raw	5	Canned in syrup	20
Fillet, fried	55	Fried	100	Plaice (fillet)	
Smoked	70	Rings fried in batter	145	Raw or steamed	25
Mandarins		Oranges		Fried in batter	80
Canned	15	Flesh only	10	Fried in crumbs	65
Fresh, with skin	5	With skin	5	Plums	
Margarine	205	Juice	10	Fresh dessert, with stones	10
Marmalade	75	Parsnips (raw or boiled)	15	Cooking, with stones	5
Marzipan	125	Peaches		Pork	
Mayonnaise	205	Fresh, with stones	10	Roast, lean & fat	80
Melon (with skin)	5	Canned in syrup	25	Roast, lean meat only	50
Milk		Peanuts		Cracking	190
Gold Top	430	Shelled or roasted, salted	160	Scratchings	185
Red Top	370	Peanut butter	175	Prawns	
Longlife/UHT	370	Pears		With shells	10
Low-fat powdered	200	Fresh	10	Without shells	30
Pasteurised/Silver Top	370	Canned in syrup	20	Prunes	
Skimmed	200	Peas		Dried	45
Sterilized	370	Fresh, raw	20	Stewed (no sugar)	25
Evaporated	45	Fresh, boiled	15	Rabbit	
Condensed (sweetened)	90	Canned, garden	15	On bone, stewed	25
Muesli	105	Canned, processed	25	Meat only, stewed	50
Mushrooms (raw)	5	Chick, raw	90	Radishes	5
Mussels		Perch		Raspberries	
Boiled, with shells	5	White	35	Fresh	5
Boiled, without shells	25	Yellow	25	Tinned, drained	25
Nectarines	15	Pheasant		Redcurrants (fresh)	5
Noodles (cooked)	35	Roast, on bone	40	Rhubarb	negligible
Nuts (mixed, roasted, salted)	175	Roast, meat only	60	Rice	
Olive Oil	255	Pilchards (canned in tomato sauce)	35	Raw	100

"One cannot think well, love well, sleep well,
unless one has dined well."

Virginia Woolf

Food & Health ~ Calorie Counting

Boiled	35
Salmon	
Raw, on bone	50
Steamed, on bone	45
Steamed, fillet	55
Canned	45
Smoked	40
Sardines	
Canned in oil, drained	60
Canned in tomato sauce	50
Sausages	
Pork, lightly fried or grilled	165
Pork, well fried or grilled	115
Pork, chipolata:	
lightly fried or grilled	165
well fried or grilled	115
Beef, fried or grilled	120
Beef, chipolata fried or grilled	120
Scampi (fried in breadcrumbs)	90
Semolina (raw)	100
Shrimps	
With shells	10
Without shells	35
Canned	25
Skate (fillet fried in batter)	55
Sole	
Fillet, raw	25
Fillet, fried	60
Fillet, steamed	25
On bone, steamed	20
Spaghetti	
Raw	105

Boiled	35
Canned in tomato sauce	15
Spinach (boiled)	10
Spring Onions	10
Strawberries	
Fresh	5
Tinned, drained	25
Sturgeon (on bone, raw)	25
Sugar	110
Sultanas (dried)	70
Sunflower Seed Oil	255
Swedes	5
Sweetcorn	
Canned	20
Fresh boiled, kernels	35
Frozen	25
Sweets	
Boiled sweets	95
Filled chocolates	130
Fudge	110
Peppermints	110
Toffee	120
Syrup	
Golden	85
Maple	70
Tangerines	
Flesh only	10
With skin	5
Tapioca (dry)	100
Tea	negligible
Tomatoes	
Canned	5

Fried, halved	20
Fried, sliced	30
Ketchup	30
Puree	20
Raw	5
Tongue (Ox, boiled)	85
Treacle (Black)	85
Tripe (Stewed)	30
Trout	
Fillet, smoked	35
On bone, steamed	25
Tuna	
Canned in oil	80
Drained of oil	60
Turkey	
Meat only, roast	40
Meat & skin, roast	50
Turnips (raw)	5
Veal	
Escalope, fried (egg/b'crumbs)	60
Fillet, raw	30
Fillet, roast	65
Venison (roast, meat)	55
Watermelon	5
Whitebait (fried)	150
Whiting	
On bone, fried	50
Fillet, fried	55
On bone, steamed	20
Fillet, steamed	25
Yorkshire Pudding (cooked)	60

Menu Suggestions

Keep a record of any favourite meals, recommended dishes or any new recipes that you try out to ensure that your imagination never fails you whether it comes to creating a gourmet extravaganza or a family dinner!

Starters

....

....

....

....

....

....

Main Courses

....

....

....

....

Menu Suggestions

Main Courses

....
....
....
....
....
....

Desserts

....
....
....
....
....
....

Complete Menu Suggestions

Starter ....

Main Course ....

Dessert ....

Notes ....

....

Starter ....

Main Course ....

Dessert ....

Notes ....

....

Starter ....

Main Course ....

Dessert ....

Notes ....

....

Starter ....

Main Course ....

Dessert ....

Notes ....

....

Starter ....

Main Course ....

Dessert ....

Notes ....

....

Starter ....

Main Course ....

Dessert ....

Notes ....

....

Special Occasion Recipes

Recipe ....

Ingredients

....
....
....
....
....
....

Method

....
....
....
....
....
....
....
....

Recipe ....

Ingredients

....
....
....
....
....
....

Method

....
....
....
....
....
....
....

Special Occasion Recipes

Recipe ....

Ingredients

....
....
....
....
....

Method

....
....
....
....
....
....
....
....

Recipe ....

Ingredients

....
....
....
....
....

Method

....
....
....
....
....
....
....
....

Special Occasion Recipes

Recipe ....

Ingredients

....
....
....
....
....
....

Method

....
....
....
....
....
....
....
....

Recipe ....

Ingredients

....
....
....
....
....
....

Method

....
....
....
....
....
....
....
....

Special Occasion Recipes

Recipe ....

Ingredients

....
....
....
....
....
....

Method

....
....
....
....
....
....
....
....
....

Recipe ....

Ingredients

....
....
....
....
....
....

Method

....
....
....
....
....
....
....
....
....

Special Occasion Recipes

Recipe ....

Ingredients

....
....
....
....
....

Method

....
....
....
....
....
....
....
....

Recipe ....

Ingredients

....
....
....
....
....

Method

....
....
....
....
....
....
....
....

Special Occasion Recipes

Recipe ....

Ingredients

....
....
....
....
....

Method

....
....
....
....
....
....
....
....

Recipe ....

Ingredients

....
....
....
....
....

Method

....
....
....
....
....
....
....
....

Special Occasion Recipes

Recipe ....

Ingredients

....

....

....

....

....

....

Method

....

....

....

....

....

....

....

....

Recipe ....

Ingredients

....

....

....

....

....

....

Method

....

....

....

....

....

....

....

....

Friends & Food Preferences

Little can be so disheartening to the cook to learn that a meal that has been hours in the preparation is poison to one of the guests – maybe he or she is a vegetarian, allergic to eggs, detests olives . . . ! Avoid uncomfortable situations by keeping a record of your friends' food preferences, and why not also make a note of any meals you have served them to avoid repetition of menus.

Friend ....

Allergies/ ....

Dislikes ....

Notes ....

....

....

....

Friend ....

Allergies/ ....

Dislikes ....

Notes ....

....

....

....

Friend ....

Allergies/ ....

Dislikes ....

Notes ....

....

....

....

Friend ....

Allergies/ ....

Dislikes ....

Notes ....

....

....

....

"Cooking is like love. It should be entered
into with abandon or not at all."

Harriet Van Horne

Friends & Food Preferences

Friend ....

Allergies/

Dislikes ....

Notes ....

....

....

....

Friend ....

Allergies/

Dislikes ....

Notes ....

....

....

....

Friend ....

Allergies/

Dislikes ....

Notes ....

....

....

....

Friend ....

Allergies/

Dislikes ....

Notes ....

....

....

....

Friends & Food Preferences

Friend ....

Allergies/ ....

Dislikes ....

Notes ....

....

....

....

Friend ....

Allergies/ ....

Dislikes ....

Notes ....

....

....

....

....

Friend ....

Allergies/ ....

Dislikes ....

Notes ....

....

....

....

Friend ....

Allergies/ ....

Dislikes ....

Notes ....

....

....

....

"The art of dining well is no slight art,
the pleasure not a slight pleasure."

Montaigne

Dinner Parties

Date ....

Guests

....

....

....

....

Menu

....

....

....

....

....

Wines ....

....

Notes ....

....

Date ....

Guests

....

....

....

....

Menu

....

....

....

....

....

Wines ....

....

Notes ....

....

Dinner Parties

Date ....

Guests

....
....
....
....

Menu

....
....
....
....
....

Wines ....

....

Notes

....
....

Date ....

Guests

....
....
....
....

Menu

....
....
....
....
....

Wines ....

....

Notes

....
....

Dinner Parties

Date ....

Guests

....

....

....

....

Menu

....

....

....

....

....

Wines ....

....

Notes ....

....

Date ....

Guests

....

....

....

....

Menu

....

....

....

....

....

Wines ....

....

Notes ....

....

Dinner Parties

Date ....

Guests

....

....

....

....

Menu

....

....

....

....

Wines ....

....

Notes ....

....

Date ....

Guests

....

....

....

....

Menu

....

....

....

....

Wines ....

....

Notes ....

....

Dinner Parties

Date ....

Guests

....
....
....
....

Menu

....
....
....
....

Wines ....
....

Notes ....
....

Date ....

Guests

....
....
....
....

Menu

....
....
....
....

Wines ....
....

Notes ....
....

Dinner Parties

Date ....

Guests

....

....

....

....

Menu

....

....

....

....

....

Wines ....

....

Notes ....

....

Date ....

Guests

....

....

....

....

Menu

....

....

....

....

....

Wines ....

....

Notes ....

....

Dinner Parties

Date ....

Guests

....
....
....
....

Menu

....
....
....
....

Wines ....

Notes ....
....

Date ....

Guests

....
....
....
....

Menu

....
....
....
....

Wines ....

Notes ....
....

Dining Out

Date ....

Location ....

Diners ....

....

....

....

Menu ....

....

....

....

....

Wines ....

....

Notes ....

....

Date ....

Location ....

Diners ....

....

....

....

Menu ....

....

....

....

....

Wines ....

....

Notes ....

....

"When a man's stomach is full it makes no difference whether he is rich or poor."

Euripides

Dining Out

Date	Date ....
Location	*Location* ....
Diners	Diners ....
....	....
....	....
....	....
Menu	Menu ....
....	....
....	....
....	....
Wines	Wines ....
Notes	Notes ....
....	....

Dining Out

Date	Date
Location	*Location*
Diners	Diners
Menu	Menu
Wines	Wines
Notes	Notes

Dining Out

Date .... Date ....

Location .... *Location* ....

Diners .... Diners ....

....

....

....

Menu .... Menu ....

....

....

....

....

Wines .... Wines ....

....

Notes .... Notes ....

....

Dining Out

Date ....

Location ....

Diners ....

....

....

....

Menu ....

....

....

....

Wines ....

....

Notes ....

....

Date ....

Location ....

Diners ....

....

....

....

Menu ....

....

....

....

Wines ....

....

Notes ....

....

"Any cook should be able to
run the country."
Lenin

Dining Out

Date	Date
Location	*Location*
Diners	Diners
Menu	Menu
Wines	Wines
Notes	Notes

Dining Out

Date ....

Location

Diners
....
....
....

Menu ....
....
....
....

Wines ....
....

Notes ....
....

Date ....

Location

Diners
....
....
....

Menu ....
....
....
....

Wines ....
....

Notes ....
....

Dining Out

Date ....   Date ....

Location ....   *Location* ....

Diners ....   Diners ....

....

....

....

Menu ....   Menu ....

....

....

....

....

Wines ....   Wines ....

....

Notes ....   Notes ....

Dining Out

Date	Date
Location	*Location*
Diners	Diners
Menu	Menu
Wines	Wines
Notes	Notes

Fine Wines

Use this section to keep a record of wines that you have tried and particularly liked (or disliked!)

Wine ....

Where Tasted ....

Comments ....

....

Wine ....

Where Tasted ....

Comments ....

....

Wine ....

Where Tasted ....

Comments ....

....

Wine ....

Where Tasted ....

Comments ....

....

Wine ....

Where Tasted ....

Comments ....

....

Wine ....

Where Tasted ....

Comments ....

....

Fine Wines

Wine ....

Where Tasted ....

Comments ....

....

Wine ....

Where Tasted ....

Comments ....

....

Wine ....

Where Tasted ....

Comments ....

....

Wine ....

Where Tasted ....

Comments ....

....

Wine ....

Where Tasted ....

Comments ....

....

Wine ....

Where Tasted ....

Comments ....

....

Fine Wines

Wine	Wine
Where Tasted	Where Tasted
Comments	Comments
Wine	Wine
Where Tasted	Where Tasted
Comments	Comments
Wine	Wine
Where Tasted	Where Tasted
Comments	Comments

Notes

Notes

Notes

Acknowledgements

The Wedding Feast by Sandro Botticelli (1444/5-1510)
Private Collection/Bridgeman Art Library, London

Still Life by Osias Beert the Elder (c. 1570-1624)
Prado, Madrid/Bridgeman Art Library, London

Still Life of Glass Goblet by Pieter Claesz (1597-1660)
Rafael Valls Gallery, London/Bridgeman Art Library, London

Still Life with Decanters by J. Rhodes (fl. 1820-40)
Private Collection/Bridgeman Art Library, London

A Still Life of Grapes Resting on a Marble Ledge by G. Van Spaendonck (1746-1822)
Rafael Valls Gallery, London/Bridgeman Art Library, London

Other images © Robert Frederick Ltd. 1996